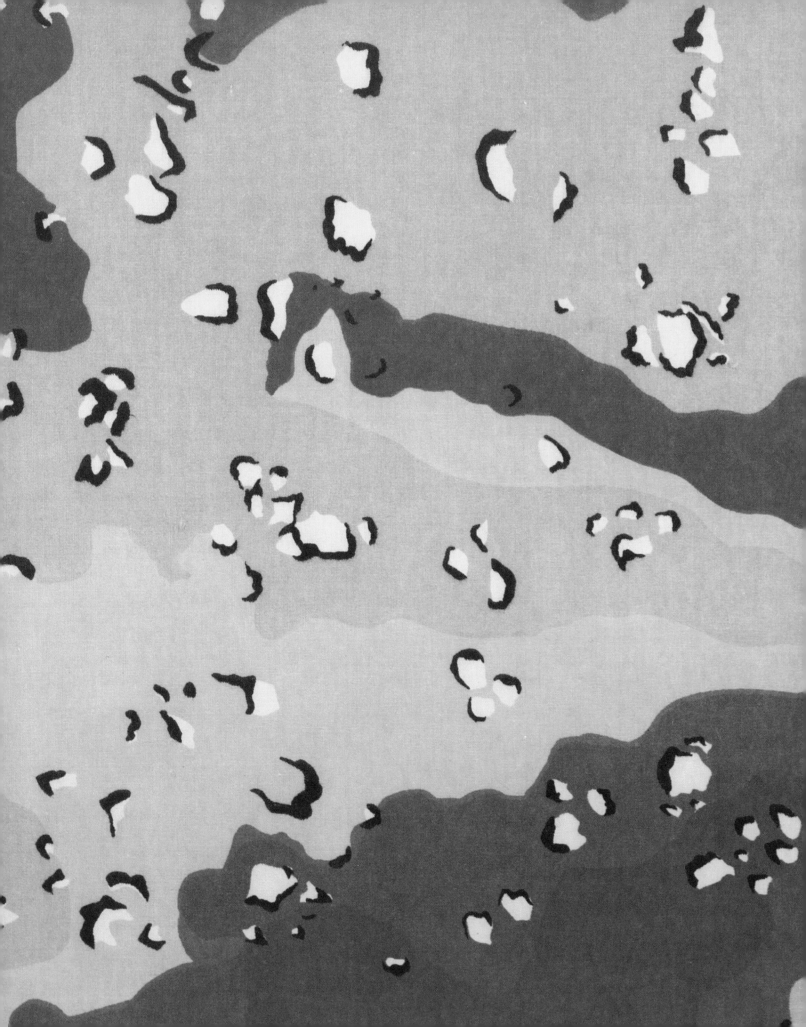

Writer: Keith F. Girard
Editorial Director: Moira J. Saucer
Publisher: Don J. Beville
Technical Advisor: Major Floyd John Johnson, III
Design: Geary, Flynn & Crank, Inc.
Photo Editing: Major Floyd John Johnson, III; Don J. Beville
Senior Production Coordinator: Nick Levay
Photography: Department of Defense; Gamma-Liaison; Marine Corps
    Association, Division of Public Affairs, Marine Corps Headquarters;
    Ross Simpson, NBC Radio Correspondent; Wide World Photos.
Color Separations: Michael's Color Service, Inc.

Library of Congress catalog number 91-072121

ISBN 0-9629648-0-8 Leather edition: ISBN 0-9629648-1-6

Produced and printed by The Fine Books Division of William Byrd Press
PO Box 27481, Richmond, Virginia 23261

Overleaf: "Hurry up and Wait." Marines awaiting transportation
ground their gear and relax as the build up continues.

This spread: "The calm before the storm." The Marines manning this
M-60 tank have the opportunity to observe a beautiful desert sunset as
they prepare for the coming night's activities.

REMEMBERING THE GULF WAR

A photographic essay with text by Keith F. Girard

Edited by Moira J. Saucer

Published by Don J. Beville,
Cadmus Communications Corporation

CONTENTS

ACKNOWLEDGEMENTS

The publisher would like to take this opportunity to express his gratitude to those whose untiring efforts have led to the creation of this remarkable book. To Lieutenant General Anthony Lukeman, USMC (Retired), Colonel L.J. Piantadosi, USMC (Retired), Colonel William V.H. White, USMC (Retired), and Colonel John E. Greenwood, USMC (Retired) of the Marine Corps Association for the support throughout the project. To Kate Stark, art director of *Leatherneck Magazine* who helped in finding special photographs at the last minute.

To Captain John Buford whose efforts led to the formation of an extensive list of Marines to interview for the book.

A special thanks to the Marines of the Division of Public Affairs, Marine Corps Headquarters who provided photographic and caption information.

I am most grateful to Major Floyd John Johnson, III of the Amphibious Warfare School, U.S. Marine Corps, who gave me the benefit of his extensive knowledge of military technology and warfare.

I also would like to thank Geary, Flynn & Crank, Inc. As designer of this book, the firm has made it a more effective and attractive publication by providing useful counsel with copy and photographic editing, proofreading and graphic styling.

My deepest thanks to Keith F. Girard who provided the words for the book under an enormous deadline. And, to Moira J. Saucer, whose diligence and skill as an editor I have good reason to appreciate.

*They shall grow not old, as
we that are left grow old:*

*Age shall not weary them,
nor the years condemn.*

*At the going down of the
sun and in the morning*

We will remember them.

*"For the Fallen"
by Laurence Binyon*

DEDICATED TO THE MARINES
THAT MADE THE ULTIMATE SACRIFICE

KILLED IN ACTION (ALPHABETICALLY)

29 Jan. - LCpl Frank C. Allen, 22, Waianae, Hawaii
1/9 CamPen

29 Jan. - Cpl Stephen E. Bentzlin, 23, Yellow Meadow, Minnesota
1/9 CamPen

29 Jan. - Cpl Ismael Cotto, 27, Bronx, New York
1st LAI CamPen

2 Feb. - LCpl Eliseo Felix, 19, Avondale, Arizona
5/11 29 Palms

27 Feb. - Sgt James D. Hawthorne, 24, Stinnett, Texas
2nd TkBn 2nd Mardiv CLJ

29 Jan. - LCpl Thomas A. Jenkins, 20, Mariposa, California
1st Combat Eng Bn CamPen

24 Feb. - Cpl Phillip J. Jones, 21, Atlanta, Georgia
3/10 CLJ

27 Feb. - LCpl Brian L. Lane, 20, Bedford, Indiana
3/7 29 Palms

29 Jan. - LCpl Michael E. Linderman Jr., 19, Douglas, Oregon
3rd LAI 29 Palms

29 Jan. - LCpl James H. Lumpkins, 22, New Richmond, Ohio
3rd LAI 29 Palms

29 Jan. - Sgt Garett A. Mongrella, 25, Belvidere, New Jersey
3rd LAI 29 Palms

23 Feb. - Cpl Aaron A. Pack, 22, Phoenix, Arizona
HqBtry 11th Mar CamPen

27 Feb. - LCpl Christian J. Porter, 20, Wood Dale, Illinois
3/7 29 Palms

29 Jan. - PFC Scott A. Schroeder, 20, Milwaukee, Wisconsin
3rd LAI 29 Palms

29 Jan. - LCpl David T. Snyder, 21, Erie, New York
1st LAI CamPen

25 Feb. - Capt David M. Spellacy, 28, Columbus, Ohio
VMO-1, MAG 29, 2nd MAW

29 Jan. - PFC Dion J. Stephenson, 20, Davis, Utah
1/9 CamPen

27 Feb. - Capt Reginald C. Underwood, 27, Lexington, Kentucky
VMA-331, MAG 32, 2nd MAW

26 Feb. - LCpl James E. Waldron, 25, Jeannett, Pennsylvania
A Co, 7th EngrSptBn, 1st FSSG, CamPen

29 Jan. - LCpl David B. Walker, 20, Flint, Texas
1st LAI CamPen

23 Feb. - Capt James N. Wilbourn III, 28, Huntsville, Alabama
VMA-542, MAG 13, 3rd MAW

DIED OF WOUNDS

26 Feb. - LCpl Troy L. Gregory, 21, Richmond, Virginia
3/14 4th MarDiv USMCR

2 Mar. - Sgt Candelario Montalvo Jr., 25, Eagle Pass, Texas
HqBn, 2nd MarDiv

Saddam Hussein

It began like most wars of aggression, with a swift and sudden strike, launched in a swirl of deception by a maniacal dictator bent on conquest and plunder.

On Aug. 2, 1990, under the cover of darkness, the elite Republican Guard of Iraqi President Saddam Hussein spearheaded the invasion of Kuwait. The attack marked the beginning of a five-month standoff that ended with the largest U.S. military operation since the D-Day invasion of Normandy in World War II.

Saddam promised to fight the "Mother of All Battles" and poured thousands of tanks and artillery and half a million troops into Kuwait to back up his threat. But the Mother of All Battles turned into the Mother of All Routs. With speed, precision, daring and courage, the United States and its allies engineered one of the most remarkable military victories in the history of modern warfare.

It was all over in 100 hours.

By the time the guns fell silent, the soldiers, sailors, airman and Marines who had participated in Operation Desert Storm could take pride in the fact that they had answered a solemn call to arms and had carried out their duties in a way that would engage the respect—and the hearts—of most Americans.

U. S. Marines beginning the process of digging in.

It was a battle that not only vanquished a dictator but also renewed America's can-do spirit. More importantly, it restored a nation's faith in itself.

This book is about the U.S. Marines who served in Operation Desert Storm. In all, more than 96,000 Marines were called to duty in the Persian Gulf. Many of them spent months in the harsh, alien environment, enduring the loneliness of a long separation from home, the desolation and bitter climatic extremes of the desert and the endless tedium that always precedes combat. Each Marine, in his or her own way, also had to confront the haunting fears that lurk within

every warrior—fear of the unknown, fear of failure, fear of dishonor and fear of death.

The attack that started it all began precisely at 0200 hours on the morning of Aug. 2. That was the moment Iraqi troops stormed into the tiny oil-kingdom and raced for Kuwait City, the seat of the royal al-Sabah family, 80 miles away. By dawn, the vanguard of Hussein's army was on the outskirts of the capital, hammering the hapless city and its people into submission with withering tank, artillery and aircraft attacks.

The Iraqi leader tried to portray the situation as an internal squabble among Arabs. The invasion, he claimed, was only a temporary move that Iraq had been "forced" to make to resolve a simmering feud over oil and territorial rights.

Hours after Iraqi troops invaded Kuwait, the Security Council of the United Nations demanded the "immediate withdrawal" of all Iraqi troops from Kuwait.

Previous page: A Kuwaiti father and son contemplate the destruction of their country and the hard future that lies ahead.

But the implications of the attack were far more ominous than that. Early on, it became clear that Saddam had no intention of relinquishing his prize. What's more, intelligence data showed that his troops were massing for a possible assault on Saudi Arabia. The oil-rich Kingdom to the south controls 20 percent of the world's petroleum reserves. If it were to fall into the Iraqi dictator's hands, he would not only gain control of world oil markets but would emerge with a boot on the throat of the world economy.

The unpredictable and treacherous dictator would be the wealthiest, most powerful leader in the Middle East, an explosive region where Hussein could play havoc with the longstanding vital interests of the U.S. and other allies. The invasion clearly threatened world peace. Moreover, it posed a direct and serious challenge to the post-Cold War leadership of the United States.

Saddam had chosen an inauspicious time to launch his invasion. It came when the world was pre-occupied with the fall of Communism in Eastern Europe and the demise of the Soviet Union as a menacing world power. In the U.S., Hussein's move hit like a cold, unexpected slap in the face.

The end of the Cold War had created a false sense of security in Washington, where Congress was busy debating deep cuts in the defense budget. If anything, Hussein proved that the world was still a dangerous and highly volatile place.

Left: Iraqi Foreign Minister Tariq Aziz at a press conference on Jan. 9, 1991.

Right: Secretary of State James Baker traveled the world seeking a peaceful solution to the Gulf Crisis.

Within hours of the invasion, President Bush had decided to draw a line in the sand. He was determined not to let the Iraqi aggression stand.

On the diplomatic front, events moved swiftly. A day after the assault, the United Nations Security Council voted 14-0 in favor of Resolution 660, which condemned the Iraqi invasion and demanded a complete and unconditional withdrawal of troops from Kuwait. The vote was an impressive display of unity by the often fractious world body, and it helped pave the way for the formation of the 38-nation coalition that ultimately opposed Iraq.

The President firmly hoped that diplomatic means and an economic embargo would force Saddam out of Kuwait. But failing that, Bush realized that the Iraqi army would have to be ejected by force.

On the military front, however, the situation was tenuous at best. Saudi Arabia was facing the most immediate threat. U.S. intelligence determined that the Kingdom was highly vulnerable to an Iraqi blitzkrieg. Major military bases at Dhahran and Riyadh, not to mention most of the country's oil-producing facilities, were within easy striking distance of the Kuwaiti border.

It was critical for the U.S. to establish a military presence in the country as quickly as possible to act as a deterrent. Saddam had to be shown that an attack against the Kingdom would be an attack against the United States. On Aug. 3, the President agreed to offer a massive deployment of air, land and naval power in the Persian Gulf. The Saudis requested that assistance two days later.

Operation Desert Shield had begun.

Initial plans called for the deployment of the 2,300-man "ready brigade," of the 82nd Airborne Division and two squadrons of F-15 fighters to provide air support. The brigade took up defensive positions around Dhahran to protect U.S. fighters and to serve as a "trip-wire" against an Iraqi attack.

The first credible defensive deployment followed a few days later, when the first of 16,500 Marines from 7th Marine Expeditionary Brigade (MEB) landed in the country. Waiting for them were heavy tanks, amphibious assault vehicles, artillery, Sea Cobra attack helicopters, support

Right: Marines digging in for possible ground war.

Below: A Marine sniper using special night vision equipment.

equipment and 30 days of war-fighting supplies. The equipment had been pre-positioned on ships based out of Diego Garcia in the Indian Ocean, about a week's sailing time from the Persian Gulf.

The ships were part of a Maritime Pre-positioned Squadron (MPS), one of three stationed at strategic points around the globe. The squadrons are designed to reduce U.S. military response time to any one of a number of world trouble spots. Without pre-positioned supplies, the deployment of Marines would have been delayed by the weeks required to move the same equipment from the United States by ship and plane.

"The planning for this type of operation had been on-going for ten years," says Colonel Marvin Floom, who oversees logistical doctrine at the Marine Warfighting Center in Quantico. "We had in the neighborhood of 50,000 Marines on the ground by the end of August. Our ability to do that kept Hussein from invading."

U.S. Marines, PFC Bruce Mallard and PFC William Ryder man their overnight positions near the Kuwait border.

Indeed, logistics proved to be one of the biggest success stories of Desert Storm. The operation involved the largest, fastest, most extensive deployment of military forces in the annals of modern warfare. By Nov. 7, the President had ordered another 230,000 troops to the Gulf to give allied forces the offensive punch they needed to take Kuwait back by force.

By mid-January, the U.S. had moved nearly nine million tons of supplies to the Saudi peninsula. Military and civilian contract aircraft flew 6,900 missions, ferrying 215,000 passengers to the war zone. Meanwhile, the Military Sealift Command had 249 ships under its control, churning the oceans in every direction to keep the supplies flowing.

On Jan. 15, the U.N.-imposed deadline for Iraq's withdrawal passed with Saddam's troops still firmly entrenched in Kuwait. Within hours, the allies mounted one of the largest air campaigns ever waged. Hundreds of warplanes relentlessly pounded military targets across Iraq and the Kuwaiti Theater of Operations (KTO). In the first 12 hours of combat, Operation "Rolling Thunder," as it was dubbed, had chalked up more than 1,000 sorties. By war's end, that number would exceed 100,000.

"Thirsty Hornet." A F/A-18 approaches a tanker for refuelling as the air war progresses. Note one of his Sea Sparrow air-to-air missiles is missing, indicating the occurrence of a possible engagement between the Marine and some luckless Iraqi pilot.

Right: Marine flightline personnel GySgt Anthony Santo, (I), Cpl Brian Stockfish, (c), and LCpl Kevin Hunt lean against the missile racks of a Harrier jump jet. The Harrier is carrying a Sidewinder-air-to-air missile, left, and a CBU at right.

With the unleashing of the air campaign, Operation Desert Shield officially became Desert Storm.

By then, the U.S. and its allies had 680,000 troops on the ground. More than 1,300 aircraft and 1,500 helicopters were in the theater along with 1,000 tanks and 2,000 armored vehicles.

The long logistical tail of Desert Storm would eventually give the allies everything they needed to retake Kuwait. But for three tense weeks in August, only a thin line of Marines stood between Saddam and the rich oil fields of Saudi Arabia.

The grunts hunkered down in defensive positions, while Saddam flooded Kuwait with troops. For a time, U.S. forces were outnumbered by a ratio of ten-to-one. The Marines were caught as it were, between the proverbial rock and a hard place. Fortunately, they had a lot of tradition to draw on.

Marines have fought their way out of more than a few tight spots since being founded in 1775 to defend the nation against marauding privateers and the warring maritime powers of Europe. Since its birth, the Corps has been an elite, cutting edge force, ready to fight anywhere, at a moment's notice. Although the technology of war has changed, the heart of today's Corps is still the tough, disciplined, well-trained individual Marine.

In World War I, Marines distinguished themselves in tough trench fighting at Belleau Wood and the Argonne Forest and won a wider role for the Corps in the post-war military. Marine operations in World War II, at places like Guadalcanal, Iwo Jima and Okinawa, are now the stuff of legend.

In Korea, the Marine landing at Inchon, a feat deemed impossible, turned the tide of battle early in war. Later, vastly out-numbered Marines fought off an onslaught of advancing Chinese, who had entered the conflict to prop up a defeated North Korea. The courageous rear-guard action made it possible to engineer the largest sea evacuation of troops and equipment in U.S. history.

For some of the Marines of Desert Storm—especially the senior leaders—first-hand experiences of the Vietnam War are still etched firmly in their minds. Obscured from the enemy by one of the most difficult terrains in the world, and often ham-strung by political constraints, the Marines battled the torrid jungle, tropical disease and a determined foe for 18 years in the longest Marine conflict in history. Despite the war's outcome, the Marines proved their mettle repeatedly at places like Hue, Khe Sahn, Dong Ha and Da Nang.

The lessons of Vietnam were not lost on military planners or U.S. political leaders. In an address to the nation in December 1990, President Bush assured the American people that the Gulf conflict would not be a protracted war. Rather, he promised a quick, massive strike that would bring the full force of allied fire-power to bear on the Iraqi army.

Indeed, Desert Storm would be unlike any other previous military operation. It would be the first real test of the Marine Corps' Maneuver Warfare doctrine, a combat strategy that integrates air and land forces and emphasizes speed and maneuver over sheer fire-power and numerical superiority.

It would be the first to fully utilize spy-in-the-sky satellites for battlefield intelligence and it would be the first conflict to employ a host of high-tech weapons, from laser-guided bombs and stealth aircraft to night-vision goggles, infrared targeting devices, cruise missiles and battlefield computers.

Marines at Tripoli, by Col Charles H. Waterhouse, USMCR.

It would also be the first real test for sophisticated, high-cost weapons systems like the M1A1 Abrams tank, the Light Armored Vehicle, the F/A 18 Hornet, the Harrier, the Sea Cobra helicopter and the Patriot anti-missile system.

By the time the Marines and other allied forces had breached the infamous "Saddam Line" in the early morning hours of Feb. 24, the U.S. and its allies were backed by the largest air, land and sea armada since World War II. More than 3,500 allied tanks were committed to the battle, and more than 2,000 aircraft were available to provide air support. At sea, the allies deployed more than 100 warships, including six giant aircraft carriers, the battleships Wisconsin and Missouri, an 18,000-man Marine amphibious force and at least one nuclear submarine.

Despite the lopsided outcome of the battle, the liberation of Kuwait was no cakewalk. Saddam had committed 545,000 troops, 4,200 tanks, 2,800 armored vehicles and more than 3,000 pieces of artillery to the fight. Most of the troops were thought to be battle-tested combat veterans of the Iran-Iraq war. Fighting from defensive positions, the Iraqi army was rated by the U.S. Army War College as one of the two or three best in the world. The elite Republican Guard,

A U.S. Marine trains for chemical warfare.

Opposite: Marine light armored infantrymen (LAI) display a captured Iraqi flag beside their own battle color. These LAI Marines spearheaded the mobile attack, conducting the "Reconnaissance Pull" operations which enabled the Marines to locate, attack, bypass, encircle and destroy their Iraqi opponents before they could effectively react to the ground offensive.

armed with top-of-the-line, Soviet-made T-72 tanks, was ranked on a par with most Western tank divisions.

Even more disconcerting, Saddam had promised to wage brutal, World War I style trench-warfare. The Iraqi defensive strategy was built around layer upon layer of defensive bulwarks, trenches, mine fields and barbed wire barricades stretching the length of Kuwait. The intent was to channel attacking troops into killing zones, where artillery and tanks positioned in the rear could rain down deadly fire, including shells laden with poison gas and possibly even biological agents.

After weeks of air bombardment, no one could accurately gauge how well the Iraqis would fight. The Marines, who were assigned the task of breaching Saddam's defenses, were also facing a host of other unknowns. Would their high-tech equipment hold up under the rigors of sustained combat? And how well would the untested, all-volunteer Corps fight?

Those questions and more were answered in 100 hours of often intense fighting. The Marines sliced through the much vaunted Iraqi defenses and reached the outskirts of Kuwait City in just three days. Along the way, they wrote their own chapter of Marine Corps history at places like the Burgan oil fields, the Al Jabar air base, Kuwait International Airport, and Al Jarrah.

Afterward, General Norman Schwarzkopf, the Allied Commander, perhaps best summed up the Marines' role in Desert Storm: "I can't say enough about the two Marine divisions," he said. "If I use words like brilliant, it would really be an under-description of the absolutely superb job that they did. (It was) an absolutely superb operation—a textbook operation." ■

Left: Capt Randy Hammond of
Dallas, Tex. destroyed the first
Iraqi T-55 tank of the war and
captured nine EPW. All total, he
killed ten tanks, seven vehicles,
three armored personnel
carriers, and three anti-aircraft
artillery guns.

Above: Marines drill in
preparation for the ground war.

President Bush and his advisors spent the critical first hours after the Iraqi invasion debating the U.S. response to Saddam Hussein's wanton act of aggression. With Iraqi troops controlling Kuwait and menacing Saudi Arabia, the President quickly approved the projection of massive force into the region.

During previous Middle East flare-ups, past administrations had sent token forces—an aircraft carrier battle group or squadron of fighters—to show U.S. resolve. But as General Colin Powell, chairman of the Joint Chiefs of Staff, noted during one National Security Council meeting, this was "the Super Bowl."

The President's decision to deploy massive force would lead to the largest marshalling of men and equipment since World War II. The Gulf War would also herald the most rapid buildup of forces in the history of warfare, a logistical feat rivaling even Hannibal's crossing of the Alps. In less than five months, the U.S. would send 480,000 troops and more than 10 million tons of supplies and equipment into battle.

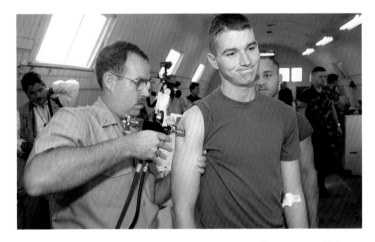

Above: A Marine Reservist receives an immunization as part of his in-processing to active duty.

Opposite: "I gotcha!" The child of an unidentified Marine corporal hangs on tight while the unit waits to board transportation to the port of embarkation.

The 6,800-man "ready brigade" of the Army's 82nd Airborne Division was the first to arrive in the region. But it was up to the Marines to land the first "heavy" defensive force. Fortunately, the Corps had been planning for just such a mission for more than a decade.

Indeed, Desert Storm would become the first full-scale test of the Maritime Pre-positioning System, a concept under development since Vietnam. This key strategic program permits rapid deployment by the use of "pre-positioned" equipment stationed on ships at strategic locations around the globe. It also operates as a key component of the Marine Air

Above: Heavy Equipment Transporters (HETs) line up to receive off-loaded equipment at a port in Saudi Arabia. These transporters were a key element in maintaining the flow of logistical material before and during the war.

SUPERPOWER MIX. U.S. Marines perform checks on their amphibious assault vehicles (AMTRACs), at a port facility in Saudi Arabia. The Soviet freighter docked in the port makes a good backdrop.

Right: Marines loading aboard LCUs in Moorehead City, N.C. on their way to the Gulf.

Ground Task Force (MAGTF) system of force projection, providing the Marines with the ability to rapidly deploy heavily armed combat troops in any number of combinations, from individual units up to all three expeditionary forces, anywhere in the world on short notice.

Depending upon the size of its ground combat element, a MAGTF usually comes in three sizes: an expeditionary unit (MEU) organized around an infantry battalion; an expeditionary brigade (MEB) with an infantry regiment as its nucleus, or an expeditionary force (MEF), based upon a Marine division. Each MAGTF comes to fight as a self-contained fighting force consisting of a command, combat, and appropriate aviation and logistical elements. The Marines' traditional ability to task, organize, or tailor a force to a given set of circumstances, rapidly deploy it with 30 days of sustainment, and fight on arrival played a major role in deterring further aggression into Saudi Arabia by Saddam Hussein. First MEF ultimately consisted of two divisions, an airwing, and a force service support group.

On Aug. 8, Lieutenant General Walter E. Boomer assumed command of the First Marine Expeditionary Force. Two days later, the MEF was ordered to the Persian Gulf. The expeditionary force included elements of the First Marine Division, the First Force Service Support Group, the Third Marine Aircraft Wing, and the First, Fifth, and Seventh Marine Expeditionary Brigades.

The MEF also included elements of the Fourth Marine Expeditionary Brigade, which included units from the Second Marine Division, the Second Force Service Support Group and the Second Marine Aircraft Wing.

Cluster bomb units being loaded onto the cradles of a trailer for transport.

By Aug. 15, the first floating warehouses of Maritime Pre-positioned Squadron (MPS) II, based out of Diego Garcia, were off-loading in Saudi Arabia, with enough beans and bullets to supply one brigade. MPS III's ships reached the Gulf from its home port in Guam in just eight days with supplies for another brigade. The rest of the expeditionary force was delivered by a 13-ship amphibious task force that steamed across the Atlantic.

In November, after the President ordered 230,000 additional troops to the Gulf, elements of MPS I, based in Hawaii, aided in the reinforcement effort. By K-Day, First MEF had grown to 96,000 troops.

The extremes of weather and wind-driven sand made ground logistics a nightmare. The windshields of low flying attack jets were quickly pitted, requiring frequent replacement. Helicopter blades had to be wrapped with adhesive tape to avoid the same fate.

"Painting a different stroke." A Marine machine gunner puts the finishing strokes of light lubricant on his M-60 machine gun.

Left: Members of a Marine artillery battery take a chow break between fire missions. Their M198 howitzer can hurl a 96-pound projectile over 20 kilometers (13 miles).

Above: U.S. Marine MP, LCpl Stephanie Bowlin stands behind an M-60 machine gun mounted on a HUMVEE vehicle.

"In the strategic sense, Saudi Arabia was probably the ideal situation," says Colonel Marvin Floom. "They had ideal port facilities."

By Aug. 21, American troops manning the ports and airfields of Saudi Arabia were working around-the-clock, jamming the docks and runway aprons with tanks, assault amphibian vehicles, artillery, ammunition, fuel and thousands of tons of food and water. Ultimately, the Marines' long logistical tail stretched all the way back to Kansas City, Barstow, California and Albany, Georgia, which are home to the Corps' major logistics centers.

At sea, an amphibious assault squadron, carrying the Fourth Marine Expeditionary Brigade made its way into the Gulf, in anticipation of an amphibious assault on the Kuwaiti coast. The 13-ship squadron, headed by the assault ship Tarawa, later linked up with a second amphibious squadron, carrying the Fifth Marine Expeditionary Brigade. By December, the two squadrons were ready to land a "division minus," complete with armor.

The trackless desert, the extremes of weather and wind-driven sand made ground logistics a nightmare. The windshields of low flying attack jets were quickly pitted, requiring frequent replacement. Helicopter blades had to be wrapped with adhesive tape to avoid the same fate, while overhaul times on engines dropped from 300 hours to 50 hours.

A typical mechanized division can consume up to 5,000 tons of ammunition, 550,000 gallons of fuel, and 80,000 meals in a single day. To move the nearly 80,000 tons of cargo required daily to sustain Desert Storm, the operation employed a fleet of 2,000 trucks.

As equipment and supplies arrived, planning for ground resupply—and transport training for negotiating the tricky desert sands—also went on "around the clock," said Staff Sergeant Jeffrey Davis, who arrived with the First Force Service Support Group. When early developed logistical strategies were finally set into motion in the heated onrush into Kuwait, the Marines involved in transporting critical supplies would operate as an almost seamless unit.

"The teamwork was unbelievable, from private through captain," said Davis. "The captain could ask anyone to do anything and it didn't matter whether or not it was their job, the work got done."

First Lieutenant Kevin Wightman, also of the First Force Service Support Group, says "We built a huge monster to support a huge monster. If you look back at what was actually occurring, it was amazing. [Achieving] the distance of support required was miraculous."

To ease logistics problems, the Marines built a vast forward supply base just south of the Kuwaiti border. Moving so close to the front was a calculated risk, but as Brigadier General Chuck Krulak, the Marines key logistics officer cogently noted: "This war is a logisti[cians] war." ∎

A Marine logistician takes a water break during loading operations. The desert heat called for upwards of five gallons per man per day to prevent heat casualties.

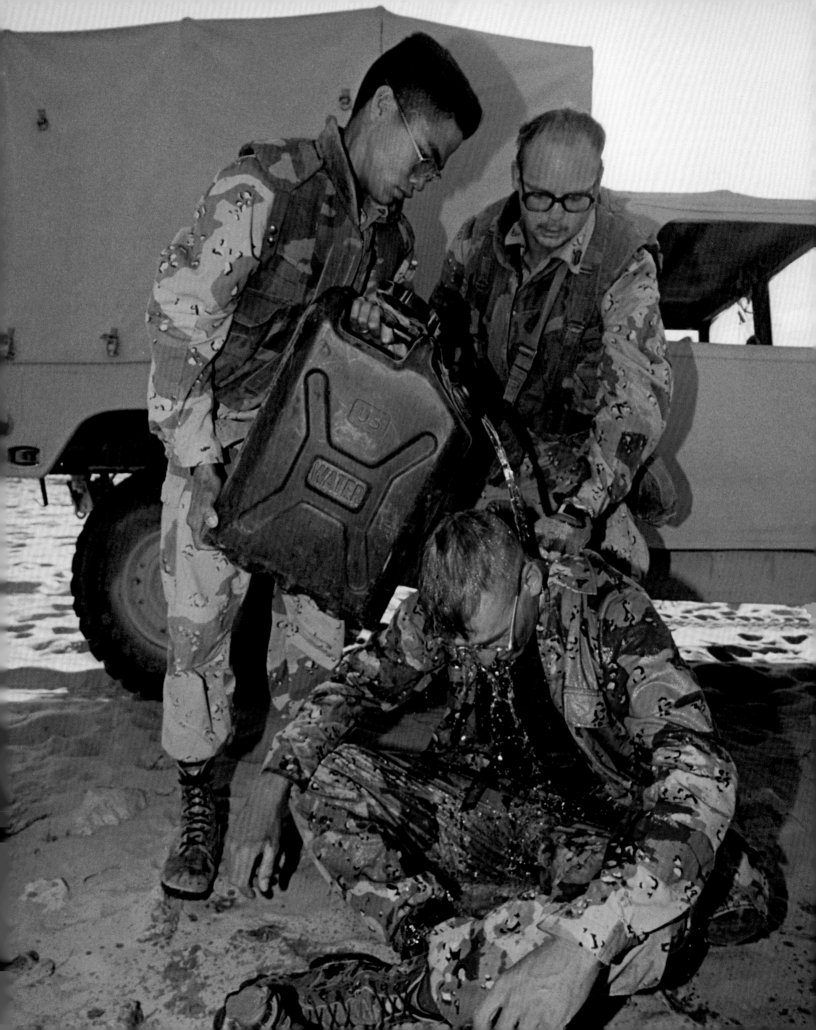

Hurry up and wait — it's one of the frustrating facts of life in war.

By the end of August, Saddam had either come to his senses, lost his nerve or made one of his classic military blunders. Whatever the case, he had stopped short of invading Saudi Arabia, and the Marines of the First MEF, who had been the first to hit the sands of Saudi Arabia, began to settle into a new life dominated by uncertainty. While some signs pointed toward peace, others pointed ominously toward war.

"Our biggest challenge was not knowing what was going to happen next," reported Third Marine Air Wing Staff Sergeant O'Kelley.

However, with each passing day, allied forces grew stronger and the likelihood of an Iraqi armor thrust south to the Saudi oil fields grew more remote. Slowly, the tension of the first few weeks gave way to relief and then boredom.

Until something happened, the "Gulf War" would become an endless cycle of training and battle drills for the Marines of Desert Shield. Rec-time did little to break the monotony. Normal liberty was out of the question. The Kingdom wanted as little cross-cultural contact as possible; thus, Saudi towns were off limits. Not that it would have mattered. Alcohol and western music are banned in Saudi Arabia and the women wear flowing black robes that cover them from head to foot.

That left the Marines to concentrate on honing their combat skills, and they sharpened them like fine steel. There were countless night patrols to get familiar with night-vision goggles and to practice night battle tactics; there were drills to learn how to call in artillery and close air support; drills to practice donning the cumbersome chemical suit, gas mask and floppy rubber boots; drills to practice trench clearing and there were countless dry-runs breaching simulated Iraqi defensive belts.

By the time the U.N. deadline rolled around, Marine commanders were confident they would slice through the Iraqi's infamous "Saddam Line" like a chain saw ripping through ponderosa pine.

During the long days of anticipation, one major spectre dominated the mind of every soldier in the theater and gripped the emotions of the American public—the horrible vision of

gas warfare. Saddam Hussein had already used chemical weapons to punish his own rebellious countrymen and his arsenal boasted both mustard and nerve gasses. Thus, each Marine was armed with nerve gas antidotes, a cumbersome charcoal-lined suit and the ubiquitous gas mask, which became a symbol of the war.

The gear was said to provide ample protection, but would it work? No one knew for sure, and that did little to ease the psychological impact of gas warfare.

On Jan. 9, 1991, Secretary of State James Baker (right) and Iraqi Foreign Minister Tariq Aziz met in Geneva, Switzerland, to discuss a possible compromise to the Gulf crisis.

While Iraq never used gas against the allies, each Marine had to come to grips with the same chilling fears. Mustard gas could sear their eyes, throat and lungs and leave them suffocating in their own fluids. Nerve gas could strike them down within minutes. For many young Marines, it was the most difficult aspect of the war to deal with.

When the soldiers weren't training, most spent their time cleaning weapons, downing chili-mac, reading mail or writing home. Some passed the hours playing pickup games of football or softball. Others jogged the beaches and still others chose to spend their time alone, thinking about loved ones, the prospect of war or just contemplating the vastness of the desert and the huge military operation unfolding around them.

As it turned out, the desert was unlike any place else in the world. What seemed like trackless expanse was actually home to countless Bedouins, marauding camels, wild dogs, scorpions as big as mice and black beetles the size of silver dollars. Some of the desert was soft and shifting. Some was as hard as concrete. And, much of the rest was as fine as talcum powder. It clogged weapons, fouled gear and somehow worked its way into every known body crevice. Some grunts swore they could even feel the grit between their teeth.

At night, the stars and the moon stood out brightly against the dark desert landscape, brighter even than the night sky at Twenty-nine Palms, where many Marines had trained for desert warfare. Off in the distance, Saudi towns lit up the night horizon like miniature sunrises.

And, everywhere, there was a constant clash of images. Bedouins, as changeless as the centuries, often crossed paths with the latest, high-tech weapons of war. Overhead, the whine of low-flying jets drowned out the howling winds and the roar of live-fire exercises echoed like thunder across the desert.

The blistering 120-degree-plus days of summer eventually gave way to the bone-chilling cold and slashing rains of winter. Although the region is only supposed to get four inches of rain a year, one 36-hour downpour in early January turned the desert into a quagmire and flooded bunkers and defensive positions at a sprawling Marine supply base near the Kuwaiti border.

Any doubts about the actuality of war, at least among the troops, were erased as the Jan. 15 deadline approached. Convoys of tanks, trucks and armored vehicles were already clogging the roads heading for the Kuwaiti border. At the Marines' forward supply base, "Lonesome Dove," long lines of soldiers waited to make one last telephone call home to loved ones before moving forward.

"What we all know is people are going to die," said one Marine. "The U.S. hasn't fought a war like this [since World War II]. There's nowhere to hide, no cover, you're just out there."

"You can only have so much anxiety and soul-searching," said one Marine Major attached to a squadron of Sea Stallion helicopters. "We've done everything we can do to prepare. Now we just have to do it." ■

Two Landing Craft Air Cushion (LCACs) bring Marine equipment ashore during Operation "Imminent Thunder." This practice landing kept the threat of an amphibious assault along the Kuwaiti coast foremost in the minds of the Iraqi defenders. The threat forced them to keep a large portion of their forces along the beaches and away from the real fight further inland.

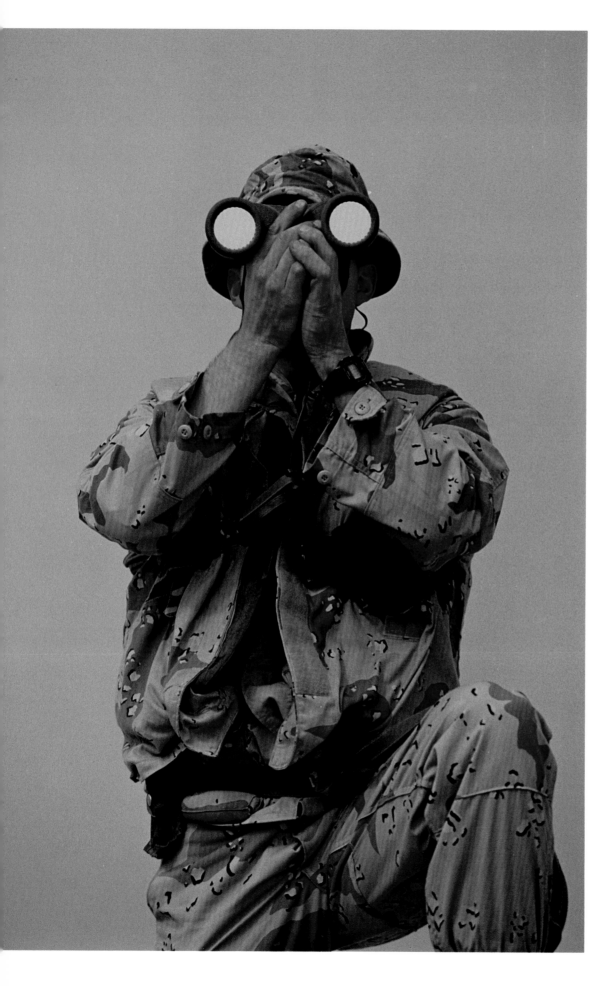

Left: A U.S. Marine uses special night vision goggles to pinpoint targets.

Top right: U.S. Marines talk on one of seven radios inside an armored assault vehicle as communications personnel direct a simulated battle. These Marines are from the 3rd Battalion, 9th Marines from Camp Pendelton, Ca.

Right: Marine LCpl Greg Schmidt, a courier, uses a motorcycle for his rounds because of its speed and maneuverability on desert terrain.

Next page: A Marine adjusts the elevation on a HAWK anti-aircraft missile launcher. The name of the missile stands for Homing All the Way Killer.

REMEMBERING THE GULF WAR. Text by Keith F. Girard. Published by Don J. Beville, Cadmus Communications Corporation. 120 pages. Photos in color. Two editions are available. The hardbound edition, Stock #9629-648-0-8, sells for $24.95. The exquisite leatherbound edition, Stock #962-9648-1-6, sells for $46.95. Add $5.00 to cover costs of postage and handling.

Many books were hastily produced during the patriotic fervor resulting from American successes of the Gulf War. Some of those books were quite good while others overlooked mistakes in order to benefit by the yellow ribbon syndrome.

This book is special. Why? Because it concentrates primarily on U.S. Marine participation. There are 112 photos in color. Beautiful. They capture the Marine spirit from Desert Shield through Operation Grizzly, Taro, G-day and Desert Storm.

The photos are beautifully displayed. Thousands of colored photographs were studied for use in the book, and the final product reflects the work of some of the world's finest civilian and military photographers. Words are held to a mini-

mum; most of the photos don't need explanations other than to identify individuals, units or equipment. There are more than a few "grabbers," and the color is vivid.

Dedicated to the 23 Marines killed in action or who died of wounds, "Remembering" begins with a simple explanation of events which caused 96,000 active and Reserve Marines to travel to serve in the Persian Gulf.

Major Floyd John Johnson III of the Amphibious Warfare School checked the copy, eliminating errors, double-checking dates and facts. Many Marines were interviewed. Photos were screened by Headquarters Marine Corps and the Division of Public Affairs to make sure caption material was correct.

Beginning with an explanation of Saddam Hussein's invasion of Kuwait, the book moves swiftly through "the Mother of All Battles."

Marines are shown as they waited, trained and sailed. They arrived, played and trained some more. And on January 16, the war began. Task Forces Ripper and Papa Bear were on the move.

In the skies, from tanks, amtracs and LAVs, artillerymen and Marines of Motor "T" swept the desert sand. And the magnificent grunts, young, eager and superbly led and trained, fought or maintained fire discipline and accepted the surrender of thousands.

The book shows it all, including the support and food distribution to Kurdish refugees.

Nearly 4,000 of Iraq's 4,280 tanks were destroyed; more than 100,000 prisoners were taken.

Of all the photos in the book, shots of homecomings, especially those of former POWs, touch the heart. Not all were joyous. Mrs. Gayle Edwards and her two sons had a tearful

homecoming as Captain Jonathan "Jack" Edwards' body was interred at Arlington National Cemetery.

"Remembering the Gulf War" is a tribute to those who served and to those who supported Marines in Southwest Asia.

General Norman Schwarzkopf summed up the Marines' role in Desert Storm: "I can't say enough about the two Marine divisions. If I use words like 'brilliant,' it would be an under-description of the absolutely superb job that they did. It was a superb operation—a textbook operation." It shows.

Tom Bartlett

SOLDIERS OF THE SEA: The United States Marine Corps, 1775-1962. By Robert Debs Heinl Jr., Col, USMC. Published by The Nautical and Aviation Publishing Co. of America. 692 pages. Stock #01. $21.95 MCA Members. $26.95 Non-members.

After being out of print for many years, "Soldiers of the Sea" has been reprinted and is once again available.

You might ask why, with other more recent Marine Corps histories available, one should buy this book which only covers events through 1962. The answer is easy. For the period it covers, the book is clearly the best. While there are other good Marine histories to be read, they pale in comparison to this one. While John Thomason is generally thought to be the best writer on Marine Corps subjects, the late Bob Heinl probably

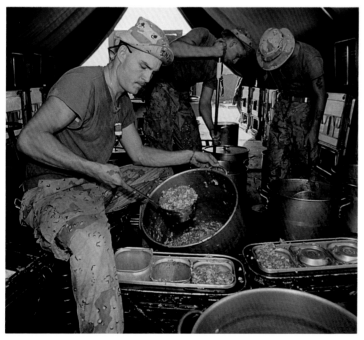

Left: Like U.S. soldiers in previous wars, Marine Sgt Timothy Kovacs uses his helmet to shave. The high-tech composite helmets seem to work as well as the old "steel pots" of the past.

Left: LCpl Cory Keeling spoons out "chili-mac" into insulated containers. The group prepares and transports over 22,000 hot meals a day.

Two U.S. Marines play baseball in front of an M-60 A1 tank. The catcher uses his flak jacket as a glove.

Right: Marines from the Second Marine Division sleep on fold-out cots next to an M-60 tank. Most Marine units have been taking part in round-the-clock exercises to prepare for the possibility of a ground offensive.

Top: SAUDI LEAGUE—
Cpl Stephanie Bowlin, the quarterback for the U.S. Marines' Wrecking Crew women's touch football team, scores a touchdown against the U.S. Navy's Desert Foxes. The Marines won 20-13.

CHARLIE COMPANY ON THE MOVE—Marines from Charlie Company, 1st Battalion, 3rd Marine Regiment, go for a late-afternoon run.

Left: Jay Leno entertains the troops.

SgtMaj Douglas Barr, with the First Marine Division, keeps up his golf practice.

Anti-aircraft artillery searches the sky in vain as precision-guided bombs and cruise missiles devastate military targets in the heart of Baghdad.

Operation Desert Storm exploded in the skies over Baghdad on Jan. 16, with a thunderous display of the terrifying wizardry of modern war. But for the soldiers of the First and Second Marine Divisions, the Battle for Kuwait would come down to an age-old contest of blood and iron.

While the world was mesmerized by scenes of Baghdad nightmarishly illuminated by the eerie incandescence of anti-aircraft tracers, the ground war was unfolding three miles from the Kuwaiti border. On Jan. 21, at 3:14 a.m., a First Division artillery unit escorted by Light Armored Infantry opened up on Iraqi positions with 155-mm howitzers.

It was the first artillery raid of the war and it marked the beginning of a deadly cat-and-mouse game. "Incoming! Incoming!" had become an almost nightly refrain along Marine lines. To counter Iraqi fire, Marine gunners moved forward, fired and withdrew before the Iraqis could respond. The tactic got the Iraqis' attention.

On Jan. 29, under the glare of a full moon, 1,500 Iraqi troops backed by at least 50 tanks launched a four-pronged attack on a front stretching from Khafji on the Saudi Arabia coast to the towns of Umm Hujul and Al Wafra, 25-miles inland. Air Force A-10s,

U.S. Marines from the Second Marine Division located just a few miles from Kuwait fire a 203mm howitzer at Iraqi positions inside Kuwait.

Left: A destroyed T-55 Iraqi tank.

Marine A-6s and Cobra gunships pounced from the sky, Marine 155-mm howitzers roared from the rear and Marine light armor unleashed a flurry of TOW anti-tank missiles. The battle, said Marine Lieutenant Colonel Cliff Myers, was "hellacious."

Saudi and Qatari troops backed by Marine artillery, attack helicopters and light armor drove the Iraqis out of Khafji after 36 hours of fighting. Two additional daylight armor attacks were repulsed at the border. From the allied perspective, the assault was a "mosquito on an elephant."

But it was revealing in one sense-- the Iraqis quit fighting well short of martyrdom. More than 500 surrendered at Khafji, a harbinger of things to come.

Marines could hardly contain their elation. " It felt good, really good," said Marine Captain Bill Wainwright, who called in air strikes throughout the night. "We kicked their asses."

The incursion would ultimately become a side-show. During the first weeks of February, Marines would step up their artillery duels and begin a series of secret cross-border incursions.

Inside Kuwait proper, the Iraqis were relying on two defensive belts to stop the Marines. The first, 12 miles inside Kuwait, was supposed to slow the advance, while the bulk of Iraqi troops, waiting behind a second defensive belt six miles away, pounced on the advancing allies.

At least three days before the massive allied ground assault, company-sized Marine units (up to 3,000 men in all) began moving into Kuwait. Marine light armor vehicles (LAV), of Task Force Grizzly and Task Force Taro, were dispatched to scout out enemy positions, probe for gaps in defenses and coordinate air and artillery strikes. Iraqi units were so befuddled by the incursions, Baghdad radio began broadcasting that the ground invasion had actually begun, even though it was still two days away.

"Upload." An ordnance loading crew attaches a Cluster Bomb Unit to one of the ordnance stations of a jet as the round-the-clock air bombardment continues.

By the 24th of February, Grizzly and Taro had punched through the first defensive line and had secured the flanks of the area where the armored and mechanized units of Task Force Ripper and Task Force Papa Bear would spearhead the drive toward Kuwait City. At 4 a.m., sappers began opening lines through the mine fields of the Saddam Line, and the Marines charged through.

The mission was two-fold: to "fix" Iraqi forces in Kuwait, while Army armor pulled an end-run around the Republican Guard in southern Iraq; and to defeat the 12 enemy divisions facing them.

The next 100 hours were an unearthly, almost surreal experience for many of the advancing Marines. Thirty-seven days of aerial bombardment had turned Kuwait into a blackened and scarred moonscape. Iraqi tanks, armored vehicles and artillery lay twisted and charred in scattered heaps. Bunkers looked like they'd been ripped apart by a tornado-like force. Still

A crew chief supervises the loading of two HARM anti-radar missiles aboard a F/A-18 of Marine Fighter Attack Squadron 451.

others were eerily intact. In one instance, plates of food and a tea pot were still sitting on a table, as if someone had just stepped out for a cup of sugar.

The foul black smoke from burning oil fires often blotted out the sun. At times, the day turned into a netherworld of ghostly twilight and the night became a black hole of darkness.

Adding to the unreality of it all were thousands of surrendering Iraqi soldiers, many starved, sick and dazed by the weeks of allied bombing. Against the surreal images of the war were juxtaposed the all-too-real sights and sounds of combat: the thumping whine of attack helicopters, the shriek of anti-tank missiles, the sudden, volcanic eruption of fire and white hot metal from exploding Iraqi armor; the whump of incoming artillery; and the staccato bursts of 25-mm chain guns.

For many soldiers, the war was an adrenalin-pumped roller coaster ride through hell. Isolated inside advancing LAVs and amphibious assault vehicles (AAVs), they strained to pick up

A formation of F/A-18 Hornets from VMFA-212, Keneoha Bay, Hawaii.

Opposite: "Con Ops." Maneuver Warfare dictates a high tempo. Here two ground crewmen demonstrate what continuous operations require, that you get your rest when and where you can, even on the flight-line.

bits of information on their tactical radios. In the fog of war, constant rumors of impending counterattacks, artillery barrages, mine field explosions and dreaded gas attacks drove up the anxiety.

The march north was peppered by sporadic enemy artillery fire and a series of short, violent skirmishes. By the end of the first day, the Second Marine Division was racing to set up blocking positions west of Kuwait City, and the First Marine division had isolated the Al Jabar Airfield, their first objective.

The advance moved so swiftly that at one point the Marines were 20 hours ahead of schedule. Battle plans had to be revised and improvised "on the fly" to take into account the rapid pace of the assault.

In the early morning darkness of Feb. 25, an Iraqi battalion launched its most threatening counterattack of the campaign from the smoke-covered Al Burgan oil fields. Enemy troops advanced to within 300 yards of Major General Mike Myatt's First Division command post, peppering it with small arms fire.

Marines aided by a swarm of Cobra gunships firing Hellfire missiles overcame the Iraqi forces, clearing the way for the final push to Kuwait City. At dawn on the third day, the First Division began a 30-mile sprint for the capital across a hellish landscape of burning oil wells. The jet-black smoke from roaring fountains of fire coated everything that passed with an oily, foul-smelling grime.

Perhaps fittingly, the Second Marine Division's drive ended southwest of the city at the end of a ghostly junkyard. To their surprise, amid the piles of rotting tires and rusted cars, they discovered a series of abandoned Iraqi bunkers, underground command posts, ammunition stores and dug-in tanks—the makings of a major Iraqi base.

The Second Division's exhausted Marines, their uniforms blackened and stained, pulled up at the junkyard to allow Kuwaiti and Egyptian troops to pass through and liberate the city. The First Division came to a halt after seizing Kuwait International Airport. Along the way they left more than 100 enemy armored vehicles, including 50 Soviet-made T-72 tanks, destroyed. At 9 p.m. on Feb. 26, a squad of reconnaissance Marines and Kuwaiti resistance fighters took control of the U.S. Embassy. The next day, they ceremoniously raised the stars and stripes.

Kuwait was liberated.

Left: An Iraqi citizen surveys the damage to an entire city block in Baghdad.

Above: "Cutting Supply Lines." By destroying most of the main bridges, the allies prevented the Iraqi army from receiving needed food, water and ammunition.

The scattered remains of an Iraqi anti-aircraft position testify to the effectiveness of the coalition bombardment.

Above: Bomb damage to a downtown Baghdad street.

Right: The "alleged" civilian bomb shelter in Baghdad. Allied intelligence indicated they were monitoring military radio messages coming from this site.

Next page: Three Marine flight personel walk past a row of Harrier jets.

THE STORM UNLEASHED
A Closer Look at Battle Tactics

On the right it begins like a football play where the quarterback changes the call at the line of scrimmage. Moving like a set back in motion, Second Division pulls off the right flank and passes behind the First Division in order to overload the Iraqi defenses further west. In Second Division's place a ghost named "TROY" portrays a force that never was, and the Iraqis report a buildup of Marine armor where none exists.

Marine infantrymen who identify with task force names like GRIZZLY and TARO exercise the skills of the hunter, infiltrating their way through Iraqi mines and defensive positions in a recurring theme of step-listen-look-hide. In three night's work they slip around and through a surrealistic landscape of burning oil wells and Iraqi defenses to secure the sites designated for breaching through the first belts. It is the third night: "G- Day."

Perhaps the Iraqis sense it coming, as the wind rustles leaves at night: something "out there," but they do not react. Their radio intercept units hear what sounds like a string of beer commercials, "BUDWEISER," "MILLER," "LONESTAR," "HAMMS" and "FALSTAFF," but the words have no meaning. Iraqi troops huddle in their bunkers and pull their blankets tighter, trying to stay warm and live through another night of bombing, artillery and psychological warfare broadcasts. To the Marine battle staffs, however, they announce the first success: all units are in their attack positions.

Special thanks to Colonel James A. Fulks for information and insight provided for this chapter in an interview.

Smoke from a burning oil well in Kuwait billows behind an Amtrac from the U.S. Marine Second Division.

Left: Mine Class—SSgt Robert Archiable explains how a U.S. M-21 anti-tank mine works to a group of U.S. Marines. The Iraqi army acquired many different types of mines from a variety of sources, including the U.S.

Above: Members of the Marines' First Force Service Support Group perform mine sweep training.

"AVALANCHE...LANDSLIDE," two words that unleash a firestorm on the Iraqis. For the Marines, fear and worry now give way to courage, esprit and superior training. In the First Division zone, two reinforced, mechanized regimental task forces named RIPPER and PAPA BEAR spring toward the Iraqi lines like tigers from ambush. The Second Division's attack goes in simultaneously. Modeling the proverbial hot knife through butter, Marine engineers cut their designated breaches in "textbook fashion" as the divisions funnel their combat power through the first belts in record time. The 100-Hour War has begun.

The Marines vindicate their Maneuver Warfare doctrine during the next three days. Accomplishing their "Commander's Intent" with "mission-type orders," "subordinate leader initiative" and an emphasis on the "moral, psychological and physical destruction of the enemy," they generate a tempo the Iraqis cannot deal with effectively.

Light armor leads with a recon-pull mission to locate the Iraqi positions and the gaps between them. Combined arms attacks are employed to suppress, bypass, envelop, and destroy the enemy. "Fast FACs" run immediate close air support missions to suppress and destroy Iraqi artillery positions. Marine artillery delivers its DPICM "steel rain" on Iraqi positions, destroying bunkers and armored vehicles alike. Battleships use Remotely Piloted Vehicles to spot the delivery of devastating 16-inch projectiles, and an Iraqi unit surrenders to an RPV. Mechanized infantry dismounts when necessary to clear Iraqi trenchlines with aggressive battle drills.

A U.S. Marine M-60 tank and an amphibious tracked vehicle explode land mines.

Far right: A convoy of U.S. Marine Second Division vehicles move past a tank equipped with a mine-plow. These troops are on the way to the front as the ground war begins.

A destroyed Iraqi armored vehicle burns along the highway leading in to Khafji.

A Marine Forward Observer Team (FO Team) directs supporting arms during the ground offensive.

Top right: "Constant Vigilance." The crew chief of this UH-1N Huey scans the ground ahead of his helicopter as it flares for landing. Any Iraqi considering taking this helicopter under fire would do well to reconsider his options because the M-2 .50 caliber machine gun next to the Marine is capable of destroying any armored vehicle lighter than a tank.

Right: An ordnance loading crew sprints toward a turning Super Cobra which has landed to receive a reload of TOW anti-tank missiles before returning to the ground war.

Far right: "Back to the nest." A CH-53E helicopter returns to the deck of an amphib ship as the convoy sails off the coast of Saudi Arabia and Kuwait.

Fierce tank battles rage throughout the days and nights: A Marine M1A1 tank company of 13 tanks destroys 30 Iraqi T-72 tanks in two minutes, at night, at a range of up to two miles. Marine infantrymen repel an Iraqi counterattack from the blazing Burgan oil field with TOWs, Dragons, and AT-4s. Cobra attack helicopters screen the flanks of the ground forces, killing enemy armored vehicles with TOW and Hellfire missiles. Everyone rounds up prisoners, sending the dazed remnants of Saddam's army to the rear as the attack presses forward.

MEF objectives are seized in short order: Al Jabar Airfield and Kuwait International Airport fall to the First Division as the Second Division closes the back door on the Iraqi forces in eastern Kuwait by seizing Al Jarrah. Coalition forces pass through the Marines on their way to liberate Kuwait City. Three days and the war is over. ■

Left: U.S. Marine armored vehicles kick up a storm of sand as they make their way through the Saudi desert on their way to the Kuwait border.

Above: LtCol Jim Mattis, (right-center) commanding officer of a 1Bn, 7th Marines, briefing his men ("The Devil Dogs") on how to destroy enemy armor in open desert with mine sleds. Ironically, the M-60 A1 hit a mine in supporting 1-7 as it breached the first Iraqi mine field in Kuwait on "G-Day."

U.S. Marines carry a wounded companion on a stretcher to a waiting helicopter during the ground war.

Opposite: "Here we go." U.S. Second Division Marines wave as they cross the border into Kuwait.

Top: A Saudi Arabian M-109 self-propelled howitzer provides fire support for coalition forces advancing with the Marines into Kuwait.

Left: Four Iraqi soldiers clutching a leaflet and white flags, surrender to Marines.

Next page: A Marine examines the remains of a burned and abandoned T-55 tank.

"Catastrophic Kill."

Top: "PSYOPS PAYOFF." Marines use the buddy system to search a surrendering Iraqi. The prisoner is carrying a psychological warfare leaflet urging Iraqi soldiers to surrender to coalition forces.

"Sorting 'em Out." Marines and their interpreters sort out this load of prisoners. Normal procedure calls for separating officers, NCOs and troops.

Right: Thousands of Soviet-made rifles captured during the fighting.

Above: Burned and abandoned vehicles litter the valley along the "Highway of Death" leading from Kuwait City to Basra. The hilly terrain in the background denied the Iraqis any escape from the roadway and the devastating coalition air attacks. Note the abandoned command and control vehicles.

Left: Marines search vehicles destroyed along the "Highway of Death." Note the futile Iraqi efforts to shield themselves from bullets and shrapnel by stuffing mattresses in and on their vehicles, a sure sign of panic and demoralization.

Above and next page: Some of the hundreds of celebrations held for coalition forces as they liberated the capital city of Kuwait.

The devastation wrought by the occupation of the Iraqi army will take years to repair.

Inset: The remains of an airliner engine sit in front of the bombed-out air traffic control tower at Kuwait International Airport.

The Environment

Despite its brevity, the Gulf War added several new pages to the terrifying art of military warfare—from the use of high-tech weapons to the refined strategies of desert blitzkrieg.

But Saddam Hussein himself added a chilling chapter that may prove his most devastating legacy to the region and to the world—eco-terrorism.

Two weeks before the U.S. and allied invasion of Kuwait, Hussein ordered the Persian Gulf flooded with oil, along with the torching of nearly all of Kuwait's 950 oil wells.

The Gulf War was the first time a combatant had resorted to the deliberate sabotaging of the environment. Although there was purported strategic design to the spill—for a time it threatened Saudi power and water plants and was supposed to hinder a possible allied amphibious assault—the environmental damage has outweighed any possible military gain.

An estimated 3 to 10 million barrels of oil gushed into the Gulf as a result of Iraqi sabotage and as much as one million barrels of oil a day are going up in flames, filling the

Left: Shell-shocked Bedouin cattle wander through a battlefield littered with abandoned vehicles, bombed-out positions and burning oil wells.

Above: An oil well fire fighter assesses the damage to one of the 500 burning wellheads sabotaged by the Iraqi army.

Kuwaiti sky with an acrid black smoke, blotting out the sun, lowering air temperatures and scattering a potentially carcinogenic black mist over the region.

Because of its size, its gently sloping sea bed and its average depth (110 feet), the Persian Gulf is a fragile ecosystem. Already, countless numbers of birds, cormorants, sandpipers, terns, ducks and curlews have been killed by the oil slick and dozens of other marine animals, including bottlenose dolphins and huge sea turtles, are threatened by it. Before it dissolves or washes away, the oil also threatens to wreak havoc with coral and plant life, a situation that could take decades to reverse.

For a time, there was even concern that the oil fires would damage the ozone layer or curtail the world's growing seasons, which in turn could lead to famine in parts of the globe. While these dire predictions haven't come to pass yet, the damage has been extensive.

The Kuwaitis must also deal with tens of thousands of unexploded mines, littering the country now and, perhaps, for years to come. Mines are still being discovered in Egypt, a major World War II battleground.

Such deliberate action to make a land uninhabitable should come as little surprise from a man like Saddam Hussein, who had no qualms about using poison gas to quell his own rebellious countrymen. But the fact remains: eco-terrorism has unleashed a new, horrific weapon of war, representing a chilling precedent with an unknown future. ∎

Top: Another casualty. This was the tanker that Iraq destroyed, creating a major oil spill in the Gulf.

Right: "Ecological Hell." The burning oil wells of Kuwait.

Far right: A young cormorant seeks refuge along a Gulf beach as Saddam Hussein's oil slick spreads along the coast.

What will the future hold for the
thousands of Kurds now left
without homes or possessions?

Marines provide support and
food distribution for Kurdish
refugees.

On a distant foreign shore, the Marines of Desert Storm paid the ultimate price in blood, sweat, toil and tears.

After months of privation and hardship, they fulfilled their mission with the courage and fighting skills that have long distinguished the Marines. Although U.S involvement in the Gulf is far from over, Operation Desert Storm has already carved a permanent place in the long and celebrated annals of the Marine Corps.

In 100 hours, the Marines of Desert Storm vanquished an entrenched and numerically superior foe known for its ruthlessness. In 100 hours, they restored a wary nation's confidence in itself and re-affirmed America's role as a world leader. In 100 hours, they erased the stigma of Vietnam and proved that a generation of young men and women had the mettle to be called *Marines.*

The allied victory was so over-whelming some have described it as a triumph of almost Biblical proportions. In all, nearly 4,000 of Iraq's 4,280 tanks were destroyed and more than 100,000 soldiers were taken prisoner. Estimates of Iraqis killed in combat range from 20,000 to 100,000.

In contrast, the U.S. lost 121 men in combat—23 of them Marines. Another 81 men were killed in non-combat accidents and 23 were listed as missing. Of the 270 Marine M-60 and M1A1 tanks that took part in the assault, only a few were damaged or destroyed, usually due to mines. In the air, the U.S. lost far fewer aircraft than military analysts had predicted.

"The loss of one human life is intolerable to any of us who are in the military," said CENTCOM Commander General Norman Schwarzkopf. "But I would tell you that casualties of that order of magnitude, considering the job that's been done and the number of forces that are involved, is almost miraculous."

On the homefront, protesters had questioned U.S. motives in the Gulf, but as the war unfolded it became clear that more than oil was at stake.

The U.S.-led invasion and the six-week air campaign that preceded it devastated Iraq's menacing war-making capability and virtually eliminated its nuclear and chemical weapons production potential. In the process, the region's chances for peace gained new life, and future generations may have been spared a far more terrible war.

Saddam Hussein proved beyond doubt that he is a maniacal dictator with little regard for peace or human life. "His [Saddam's] was an army that came to Kuwait for one reason," said Marine Brigadier General Paul Van Riper. "To loot and pillage."

Lieutenant General Walter E. Boomer led the first convoy of Marines into Kuwait City. The mindless destruction, he would later say, overwhelmed him. In the seven-month occupation, nothing escaped the Iraqi plunderers. They torched government buildings, looted shops and ransacked homes. Even zoo animals were slaughtered.

More heinous yet were the gruesome tales of rape, murder, brutality and torture, which left thousands of Kuwaitis dead or missing. If any solace can be found in this grim tableau of death and destruction, it's in the spirited Kuwaitis who valiantly resisted the invaders and in many cases risked their lives to protect others.

When the Marines finally entered the city, they were greeted with a delirious jubilation unequalled since the liberation of Paris in World War II. Thousands of shooting, cheering, flag-waving Kuwaitis filled the streets. For the Marines who were there, the joyousness of the day was only exceeded by the realization that their thoughts—finally—could turn toward home.

On Saturday, March 9, a contingent of Marines from Camp Pendelton, the first to return home from the Gulf, marched in tight order onto the base's parade deck. The men paused for a solemn moment, then broke ranks and rushed into the waiting arms of family members and friends. The men had marched off to war unheralded from the same parade ground more than seven months earlier: their mission and fate unknown. Almost two months later, their brethren in the Second Marine Division returned to North Carolina.

They returned to a hero's welcome.

Polls showed that the American public overwhelmingly supported the war in the Gulf and expressed unprecedented support for the troops. For the most part, even protesters opposing U.S. policy in the Middle East expressed support and respect for those called to fight.

The Marines hugged one another. They hugged their loved ones. And, they hugged their children, who clung tightly to arms and legs, as if to say, *never again.* For many the flood of emotions turned into a torrent of tears, laughter and exultation. A group of servicemen formed a small circle and prayed. Others talked excitedly about what they had missed the most in the

barren desert. Not surprisingly, they missed the simple things of life: green grass, pizza, cold beer, laughing children, a sunny afternoon with nothing to do.

At other bases across the U.S. similar scenes were played out time and time again, as the men and women of Desert Storm returned home.

Homecoming for Marine POWs. Left: LtCol Clifford M. Acree and his wife, Cindy, rejoice upon his return. LtCol Acree was an OV-10 Bronco pilot with Marine Aerial Observation Squadron-2.

Inset: Chief Warrant Officer Guy Hunter with wife Mary.

Mrs. Gayle Edwards holds the hands of son Bennett, left, and Spencer, during the funeral for her husband at Arlington National Cemetery. Seated at left rear is her daughter Adrianne. Marine Capt Jonathan "Jack" Edwards was killed while flying a support evacuation mission.

Wearing his father's wings and Desert Storm button, Bennett Edwards watches as the flag that draped his father's ashes is folded during the funeral.

For the 23 Marines who died, there was a homecoming too. . . a homecoming of
dress-blue uniforms, of folded flags and quiet tears. A homecoming of bowed heads, grieving
widows and solemn prayers, of young children who barely understood the meaning of war
but knew all too well that their fathers or their mothers had come home for the final time.

Of them, it can be said, they paid the ultimate price to be a Marine.

PHOTO CREDITS

AP/Wide World Photos: Dust Jacket, 10, 25, 27, 33, 36 (bottom), 43 (right), 46, 47, 48, 50, 51, 54, 55 (top, bottom right), 56, 57, 58, 59, 61, 65, 74, 75, 76, 77, 78, 79, 80, 81 (top), 84, 85, 86, 87, 88, 116, 117

DOD: 6, 7, 19, 45 (inset), 92, 93, 94 (bottom), 95

Gamma-Liaison: 8 (Gilles Saussier), 14, 15 (Richard Vogel), 18 (Kurt Waldheim), 20, 21 (L. VanDer Stockt), 22 (Jon Simon), 23 (Apesteguy-Duclos-Morvan), 24 (Georges Merillon), 30 (Eric Bouvet), 35 (Bob Riha), 42 (Georges Merillon), 52 (Apesteguy-Duclos-Morvan), 55 (bottom left, Georges Merillon), 62, 63 (L.VanDer Stockt), 64 (Noel Quidu), 70, 71 (top, Noel Quidu), 72, 73 (Noel Quidu), 81 (bottom right, Georges Merillon), 82 (Chip Hires, Georges Merillon), 89 (Chip Hires, Georges Merillon), 90, 91 (Gilles Bassignac), 94 (top, Chip Hires, Georges Merillon), 96, 97 (top, Gilles Bassignac) 98, 99 (Gilles Saussier) 100, 101 (Gilles Bassignac), 102 (L.VanDer Stockt), 103 (Noel Quidu), 104 (bottom, L.VanDer Stockt), 105 (bottom, Georges Merillon), 106 (inset, Chip Hires), 108-109 (Marc Deville), 110-111 (Douglas Burrows), 114 (Douglas Burrows), 118 (F. Carter Smith).

Official U.S. Air Force Photo: 34, 68 (SSgt Scott Stewart ,USAF)

Official U.S. Marine Corps Photo: 1, 2, 3, 4, 5,13, 26, 31, 36 (top), 37, 39, 40 (bottom), 40-41 (Capt Rick Mullen, USMC), 45 (left), 53, 60, 66, 67, 71 (bottom), 83 (all photos), 105 (top), 115 (inset).

Ross Simpson, NBC: 24 (bottom), 32, 85 (bottom right), 120

USN PHI Scott Allen: 38

USN CW0 2 Ed Bailey: 97 (bottom)

Col Charles H. Waterhouse, USMCR: 28, 29

COLOPHON

Published by Don J. Beville, Cadmus Communications Corporation
Designed by Geary, Flynn & Crank, Inc.
Composed on Macintosh IIsi in PageMaker 4.0 with heads in Univers 67 and text in Univers 57 and Sabon, output by William Byrd Press
Printed by The Fine Books Division of William Byrd Press on Westvaco Celesta Gloss 100 lb text with end paper on Howard Linen 65 lb cover

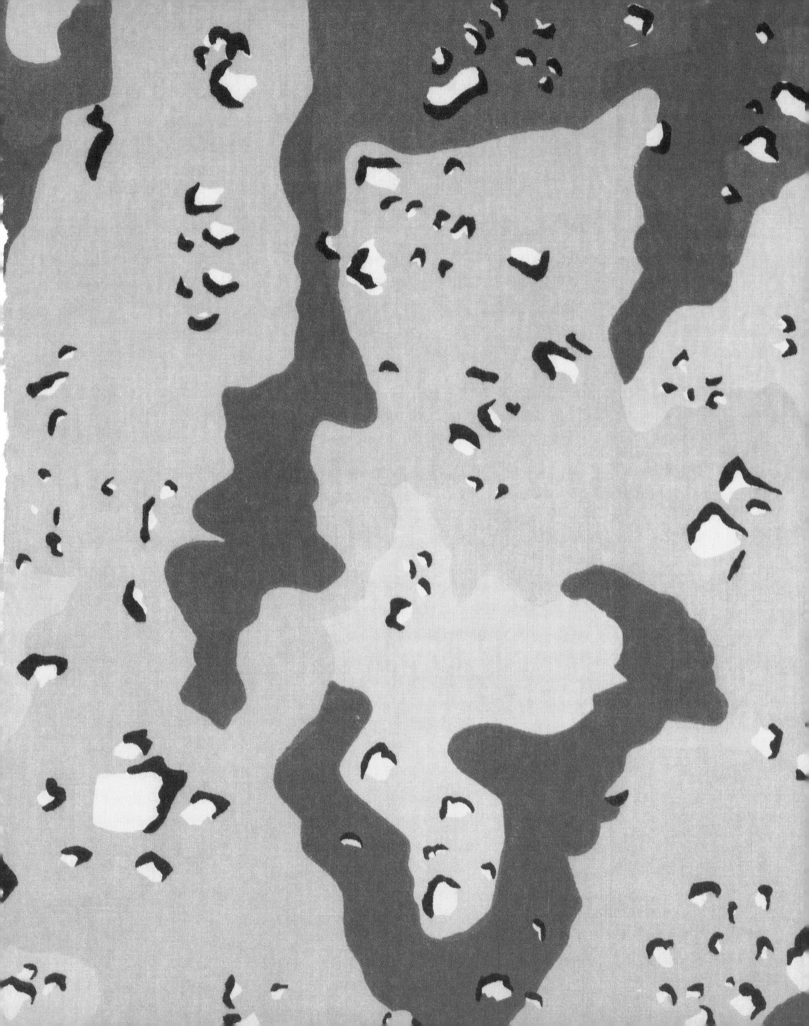

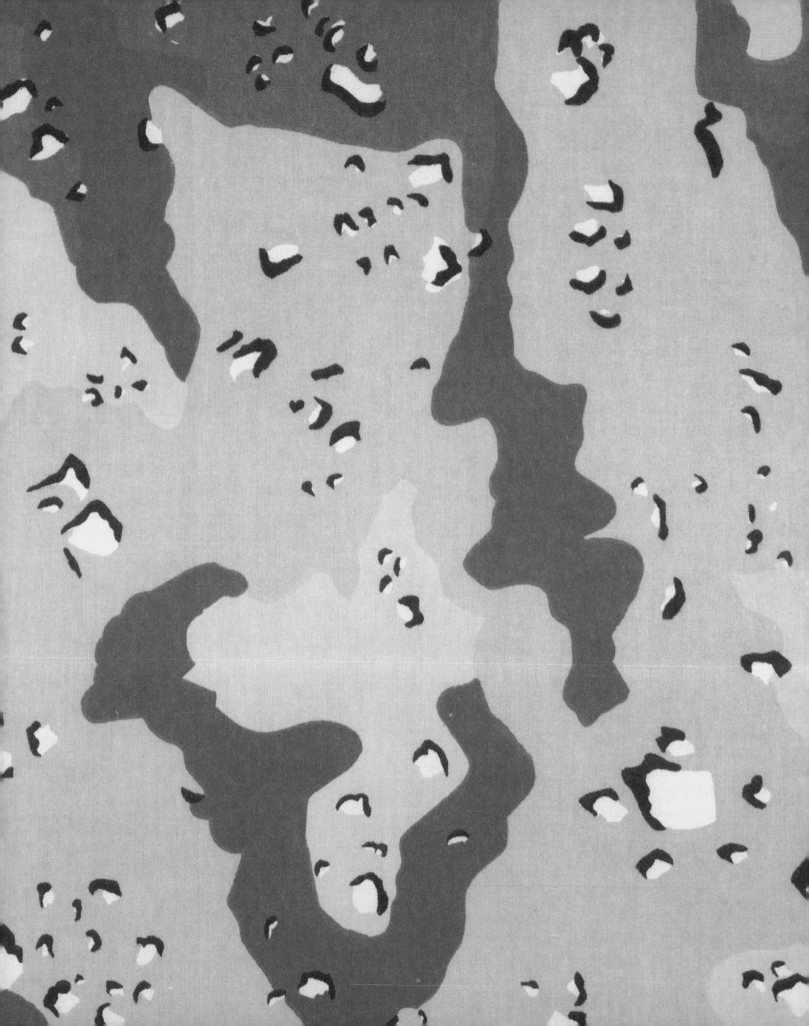